Original title:
Maple's Midnight Murmurs

Copyright © 2025 Creative Arts Management OÜ
All rights reserved.

Author: Clara Whitfield
ISBN HARDBACK: 978-1-80567-283-8
ISBN PAPERBACK: 978-1-80567-582-2

Twinkling Lights Amidst the Foliage

Amidst the leaves, a glow so bright,
Fairies dance, what a silly sight!
Twilight giggles, shadows play,
Who knew trees could join a ballet?

Squirrels debate on holiday cheer,
Hiding acorns, with a deer near.
Chubby rabbits roll on the grass,
While owls crack jokes of the past.

Gossamer Threads in Branches High

In webs of laughter, spiders weave,
Silly jokes they surely believe.
Grab a snack, the ants are near,
Join the fun, let's give a cheer!

A raccoon juggles acorns with flair,
While a squirrel's got nuts everywhere.
The moon watches, amusement clear,
As the forest fills with rambunctious cheer.

A Canvas of Color in the Moonlight

Colors splash across the scene,
A nightly party, quite the routine.
Grass stains and giggles all around,
Nature's jesters, fun unbound!

Goblins snicker in shades of green,
As ghoulish pranks grow ever keen.
Who knew the woods could be this spry?
Chasing shadows as owls fly by!

The Choreography of Covered Grounds

Leaves rustle with a rhythmic flair,
Underfoot now, a colorful layer.
Tap your toes, don't be shy,
Join the crunch as we twirl and fly!

The wind joins in with a lively tune,
Dancing freely under the moon.
Bouncing now, we leap and bound,
In nature's jest, pure joy is found.

Whispers Beneath the Autumn Canopy

In the hush of night, leaves giggle,
A squirrel dances, oh so sprightly.
Beneath glowing stars, they wiggle,
Chasing shadows, ever lightly.

A raccoon with mischief in eyes,
Juggles acorns, what a show!
While owls hoot with surprised cries,
At the antics of the woodland glow.

Secrets of the Starlit Grove

The pine trees gossip, soft and low,
About the critters lurking near.
A bunny whispers, 'Did you know?'
The raccoon stole my last carrot, dear!

Mice play poker under the moon,
Cheating fiercely, tails entwined.
A fox nearby hums a tune,
'Who knew woods could be so unrefined?'

Nocturnal Conversations Among Leaves

A hedgehog grumbles, 'Shh, be quiet!'
While crickets chirp their serenade.
A firefly glows, sparks the riot,
With laughter, the forest's masquerade.

The owl rolls its eyes, takes a nap,
Dreaming of fish that glide and swirl.
A raccoon plans a midnight trap,
To snag the cat who gives a whirl.

Echoes of the Dusk-drenched Woods

The trees sway, whispering jokes,
As porcupines crack puns, oh so bright.
The wind carries their playful pokes,
While shadows twirl in the pale moonlight.

Bats swoosh by, creating a ruckus,
Squeaking tales of daring flight.
Foxes laugh at the scenes, so ludicrous,
In the woods woven with whimsical night.

The Velvet Whisper of Night-blooming Trees

Under a blanket of stars that twinkle,
Night's fancy dance makes the shadows sprinkle.
A raccoon plays dress-up, a squirrel sings loud,
While owls throw a bash, gathering a crowd.

They shuffle and scuffle, with no time for sleep,
A mischief of critters, in laughter they leap.
In whispers of velvet, the moon starts to glow,
While crickets applaud the wild midnight show.

Enigmatic Tones of Twilight Breezes

The breeze carries secrets, a tickle, a tease,
With giggles of fireflies, joy rides the trees.
A ghost with a giggle joins in on the fun,
As shadows engage in a dance on the run.

With whispers of mischief that float through the night,
The bushes all chuckle, the trunks feel just right.
In twilight's embrace, where oddities play,
Who knew the night could be such a ballet?

A Symphony of Orange and Gold

Leaves rustle softly, a quirk in the air,
With oranges and golds, they gather to share.
The critters are cunning, the frights are a farce,
As squirrels rehearse for their grand autumn spars.

In this symphony bright, the laughter is rich,
While pumpkins all whisper, 'We're serving a witch!'
A comedy classic, beneath the bright moon,
As nightfall brings antics that make the heart swoon.

Tales from the Twilight Canopy

Atop the stout branches, the stories unfold,
With giggling critters, and tales to be told.
A raccoon in pajamas recounts a wild tale,
While owls, in bow ties, sip tea without fail.

They chuckle and chortle, with all of their might,
As shadows dance past in the soft silver light.
These tales of the twilight, where giggles are free,
Are woven with joy from the rich tapestry.

Whispers of the Harvest Moon

The pumpkins giggle in the night,
As shadows waltz in the pale moonlight.
A scarecrow struts, all decked in flair,
While owls discuss how to fix their hair.

The cornfield whispers, 'Why so shy?'
As crickets chirp their lullaby.
The apples chuckle on the tree,
'We're ripe for mischief, come and see!'

Hidden Harmonies Beneath the Stars

Stars wink above, a celestial show,
As squirrels plan a midnight row.
Moonbeams dance on leaves so bright,
While fireflies plot their next flight.

A raccoon sings with a scratchy voice,
'Let's all gather, make some noise!'
The night is young, let's all partake,
In mischief under the giant lake.

The Soft Sentiments of Autumn Nights

Breezes tease the trees with flair,
While hedgehogs scurry without a care.
Acorns plop with a tiny thud,
Kicking up a giggling flood.

The wind whispers secrets, soft and sly,
As geese honk out their battle cry.
A moonlit party, wild and free,
Join the fun of autumn's spree!

Tales Beneath the Shimmering Sky

Beneath the sky, a turtle tells,
Of wiggly worms in autumn swells.
'Why are we slow?' they ask with glee,
The answer's lost in a falling leaf.

With stars as guests, the night unfolds,
As laughter echoes, a joy untold.
Crickets lead a cheeky dance,
While everyone joins in with a prance.

Embracing the Octobers of Yore

Leaves fall like socks in a spinning dryer,
Squirrels plot how to become the high-flyer.
Ghosts in sweaters, they dance all around,
While cider spills, making puddles on ground.

Jack-o'-lanterns grin with glee at the fright,
Scaring the wise owls who stare into night.
Footsteps crunch like popcorn underfoot,
Autumn's party, who knew it was so cute?

The Soft Hush of Twilight's Kiss

Crickets tune up for a nightly parade,
While shadows tiptoe in the twilight shade.
A raccoon struts by in his winter coat,
He's the true fashionista, take a note!

Moonbeams giggle as they weave through the trees,
Whispering secrets that float on the breeze.
Each twig snaps like a silly little joke,
Nature's slapstick, without a stroke!

Constellations Amongst the Branches

Stars poke their heads through leaves like shy friends,
They chatter with critters on which fun descends.
A raccoon calls out, "I see the Big Dipper!"
But leaves rustle back, "You're such a poor flipper!"

The owls are hooting like they tell tall tales,
While bats swoop down, leaving giggles like gales.
Comets contest who can glow the most bright,
Nature's 'Show Off' gathering tonight!

Conversations in the Quiet Grove

Beneath the branches where silence is sweet,
A squirrel debates if he's faster on feet.
The wind nods along, being quite the sage,
While acorns tumble like news off the page.

A hedgehog ponders, "What's next for my kind?"
"Salads or snacks?" chirps a bird, rather blind.
Each critter chuckles, sharing thoughts with flair,
In the quiet grove, laughter fills the air!

Enigmatic Embrace of Nature

In the cloak of night, squirrels chatter,
As shadows dance beneath the moon,
A raccoon in sunglasses, what's the matter?
He's planning a party, but starts too soon.

The owl hoots gossip, spreading the cheer,
While crickets hold court with their tiny bands,
The frogs join the fun, forget their fear,
And the fireflies glow like tiny strands.

Twilight's Glimmer on Leafy Canvas

The leaves paint smiles against the sky,
With laughter of breezes, playful and bright,
A squirrel in a bow tie dashes by,
Declares the night party, oh what a sight!

The mushrooms wear hats, all fluffed and neat,
They tap dance together, what a delight!
A toad gives a speech, quite bittersweet,
While raccoons serve snacks under starlight.

Reflections in the Stillness of Night

In twilight's grip, the pond reflects cheer,
A turtle spins tales while cracking a grin,
Fish throw a rave, splashing, my dear,
And a heron in shades is ready to spin!

The moon winks down, quite the voyeur,
As shadows prance under branches so low,
A dance party forms, joining near and far,
With whispers of laughter and soft, gentle glow.

Subtle Songs of the Forest Floor

Beneath the pines, a band starts to play,
With ants on tambourines, buzzing along,
The squirrels conduct, in a nutty way,
As crickets strum softly, joining the song.

Mossy mushrooms wiggle, caught in the beat,
While a hedgehog rolls in, all dressed up neat,
The forest is lively, oh what a treat,
With giggles and grins, it's an evening sweet!

Beneath the Boughs

Under the trees, where shadows dance,
Squirrels hold meetings, plotting their chance.
A raccoon slips by, with snacks to bestow,
While critters exchange jokes, and laughter will flow.

The owls are exchanging their secrets so dear,
With jokes full of hoots that you can barely hear.
A fox rolls his eyes at the bad puns all night,
And chortles along, in the pale moonlight.

Stories Unfold

When night blankets all, tales begin to spin,
Each creature a storyteller, with a mischievous grin.
A snail shares adventures, though it takes him a while,
While the crickets add rhythm, with a syncopated style.

The fireflies blink, like winks in the dark,
As frogs croak their tales, adding their own spark.
With giggles and guffaws, the night becomes bright,
In this quirky theatre of shimmering light.

A Tapestry of Nightly Whispers

In the hush of the night, whispers fill the air,
A hedgehog tells stories with pointed flair.
A raccoon recites, with a dramatic pose,
While everyone chuckles at the punchline he chose.

Mice scurry about, taking notes with delight,
As shadows grow longer, embracing the night.
With giggles and snorts, the moon lends an ear,
To the wild, blended tales we all hold so dear.

Symphony of the Falling Leaves

Leaves drift from branches, a comedic ballet,
They twirl like a dancer, then waltz far away.
An acorn rolls past, like a runaway car,
And laughter erupts from a critter-filled bar.

A squirrel's on stage, in a leaf-draped tux,
He juggles and jests, amidst all the yucks.
While raindrops applaud, with a splat and a drop,
Nature's own concert, that never will stop.

Charmed by the Nocturnal Quarters

In corners and nooks, the night feels alive,
Where everyone's chatting, and gossip can thrive.
A chipmunk critiques the latest tree style,
While a bat shares the news, with a wink and a smile.

The wind plays a tune, with a rustle and sigh,
As owls throw a party, just giving it a try.
With punchlines delivered by starlight above,
In this quirky corner where laughter is love.

Hushed Sounds of Nature's Heartbeat

The owls are hooting with delight,
Squirrels casting shadows in the night.
Beneath a blanket of sparkling stars,
Crickets chirp as if they're in bars.

A fox sneezes, breaking the peace,
The moonlight dances, never to cease.
Bugs on a mission, a tiny parade,
Even trees giggle; they're never afraid.

Rustling Secrets in the Dark

Listen closely, the leaves conspire,
Whispers of giggles from creatures they hire.
A raccoon wearing a mask on its face,
Is rummaging through with mischievous grace.

The wind tells jokes as it sweeps by,
It drags the clouds, with a playful sigh.
The shadows are plotting the next little prank,
While stars snicker at secrets they bank.

A Symphony of Amber Whispers

Grasshoppers chirp, conducting the show,
With voices so bold, they're stealing the flow.
As fireflies flicker their tiny rear lights,
They argue about who shines the most bright.

A bear in the corner is tap-dancing well,
To the rhythm of night, casting a spell.
Everyone's clapping, even the frogs,
As night deepens, they break into blogs.

The Enchantment of Evening's Glow

Evenings are filled with a magical play,
Where shadows and giggles come out to sway.
A raccoon in a hat spins tales of the day,
While night critters join in for a grand ballet.

The owls have snacks—who knew they could bake?
With treats made of twigs and a sweet honeysuckle shake.
Every hollow sounds like a giggling spree,
In the night's cozy arms, we all feel so free.

Veiled Messages in the Evening Air

Whispers float on a breeze,
Silly secrets and wild ideas.
Fireflies blink like gossiping stars,
While shadows dance and play guitars.

One squirrel steals acorns with flair,
Another declares, "That's just not fair!"
As moonlight giggles at their chase,
Nighttime's a circus, full of grace.

Crickets and the Chorus of the Night

Crickets chirp in tune, so bright,
Creating mischief in the night.
A frog joins in with a ribbit sigh,
While owls roll eyes and wonder why.

The wind sings low, a funny hum,
As bushes rustle, a knock at the drum.
Creatures gather for their late-night show,
With jokes of dirt and seeds they sow.

Voices of the Harvest Moonlight

Under the glow of a chuckling moon,
Goblins and ghouls waltz in bloom.
Pumpkins grin with toothy glee,
While raccoons plot a sugar spree.

A scarecrow yawns, sharing tall tales,
Of windblown adventures and silly flails.
The cornfield whispers words so sly,
Joking with owls passing by.

Murmurs of the Woodland Spirits

In the woods where giggles reside,
Pixies flit with mischief as their guide.
Tree trunks chuckle at squirrel's tricks,
While mushrooms giggle like little flicks.

Beneath the ferns, there's laughter loud,
A dance of shadows, a joyous crowd.
Even the brook murmurs with glee,
Sharing secrets too silly to see.

Hints of Cinnamon in the Air

A squirrel in a scarf dances round,
While leaves play tag upon the ground.
The moon's a pie on a silver plate,
As fireflies giggle at their fate.

A raccoon dons a cheeky grin,
Searching for goodies tucked within.
Each whiff of spice draws critters near,
They'll party hard, or at least, they cheer!

The pumpkins wink in orange hues,
Sharing tales of mischief with the blues.
Beneath the stars, the laughter swells,
With shadows weaving nutty spells.

So join the fun, throw cares away,
In this sweet night, let us all play.
For in the dark, the jokes unfold,
Hints of cinnamon, brave and bold.

The Breath of Nature's Night

A nightingale sings with a twist,
Her voice is one you can't resist.
A breeze blows in, soft as a kiss,
Tickling the trees, oh what a bliss!

The owls in tuxedos share a laugh,
Deciding who of them is daft.
While crickets compete in chirpy song,
Claiming their rhythm is never wrong.

The stars giggle, that's their delight,
Winking at critters, hearts so light.
Each shadow dances, sways, and twirls,
In nature's ball, all joy unfurls.

For when the sun bids day goodbye,
The forest transforms, oh my, oh my!
With antics sweet and laughter bright,
We breathe in deep, embracing night.

Fables Spun Beneath the Oak

In the shade, where stories dwell,
A wise old turtle weaves his spell.
With each slow word, the giggles rise,
As critters listen with wide-eyed sighs.

A sly old fox joins in the fun,
With tales of tricks that never shun.
The bumblebees buzz, while ants parade,
Enjoying the fables that are laid.

Nighttime jesters hop around,
Witty dialogues in whispers sound.
Even the shy hedgehog joins the play,
Who knew there'd be such fun today?

So gather 'round, you beasts and bugs,
For laughter's warmth is now the hugs.
Beneath the oak, the magic flows,
In this canopy, the whimsy grows.

Dreamscapes of the Whispering Woods

The woods at night are full of cheer,
With mushrooms glowing, oh so clear.
A laughing brook runs wild and free,
Sharing secrets with a bumblebee.

The pixies scatter, causing glee,
While ants march to a mock parade spree.
The owls watch with bemused delight,
As creatures frolic in the moonlight.

A glowing toadstool holds a ball,
Where woodland friends all dance and sprawl.
With twirls and hops, they spin about,
In this dreamscape, none have a doubt.

So close your eyes and drift away,
To the woods where the night loves to play.
In every rustle, every sigh,
Lies a world where laughter will fly.

The Lullaby of Leafy Hues

The leaves dance in the gentle breeze,
Whisper secrets among the trees.
A squirrel tells a cheeky joke,
While owls hoot, and shadows cloak.

A toad croaks a song of delight,
As fireflies glow, oh what a sight!
The crickets laugh, they really shine,
In this leafy realm, all is divine!

The branches sway, all in a twirl,
A blush of colors starts to swirl.
The moon grins wide, a cheeky glow,
As night unfolds its whimsical show.

So snuggle close, and lend an ear,
To the laughter that spirits here.
In leafy hues, we find our glee,
A night of joy, wild and free!

Treetop Tales in the Dark

High above, the branches sway,
As critters plot their night's ballet.
A raccoon dons a silly hat,
While fireflies twirl like acrobats.

A fox whispers tales to the moon,
Of sneaky deeds, and mischief's tune.
An owl chuckles, "Oh, what a laugh!,"
As shadows play on the grassy path.

The bats swoop low, a funny sight,
Chasing their shadows in the night.
A playful breeze joins the dance,
In this treetop party, take a chance!

So join the fun, don't be forlorn,
In the night's embrace, we are reborn.
With tales in tow, we laugh and spark,
Under twinkling stars, a quirk in the dark.

Nostalgic Whispers of the Woods

Amidst the woods, a chuckle sounds,
Echoing softly from the grounds.
A deer prances, with such flair,
Wearing wildflowers in its hair.

The trees gossip in hushed glee,
Sharing stories of you and me.
A chipmunk winks and strikes a pose,
With acorns as its stylish clothes.

The brook giggles, bubbling along,
While frogs join in with a rhythmic song.
A squirrel rolls, a comic feat,
In this old forest, life is sweet!

So take a moment, breathe it in,
These woods are where the laughs begin.
With whispers of joy, nostalgia spins,
In the heart of nature, everyone wins!

Flickering Shadows of the Night

In the dark, the shadows play,
With twinkling lights that shoo away.
A raccoon jests, "I'll steal your snack!"
While bunnies hop, their little pack.

The chilly wind tells funny tales,
Of frosty nights and frolicking snails.
A lizard jokes, "I'm quite the star,"
As he struts past, not very far.

The stars twinkle with cheeky grins,
Watching over raucous sins.
A night of fun, a splendid sight,
In flickering shadows, we find delight.

So raise a toast to the moonlit scene,
Where joy abounds and laughter's keen.
In this playful night, let's make a fuss,
With flickering shadows, join the bus!

Nightfall's Gentle Caress

When shadows stretch and yawns take flight,
The owls wear glasses, oh, what a sight!
Crickets sing louder than a grandma's tale,
As squirrels throw acorns and begin to scale.

The breeze tickles leaves in a playful dance,
While raccoons wear masks, caught in a trance.
The moon laughs bright with a silver grin,
As nighttime pranksters begin to spin.

Melodies from the Forest Floor

Beneath the pines, a band takes stage,
With woodpeckers drumming, wild and sage.
Squirrels strum acorns like little guitars,
Creating a symphony beneath the stars.

A fox leads the chorus, funny and spry,
While rabbits tap dance, oh me, oh my!
The forest giggles beneath the moon's light,
As critters come out, oh what a sight!

The Calm of Autumnal Nocturnes

In the hush of night, the leaves start to snack,
Crunchy delights in a comical pack.
The bats play tag, flapping in style,
While the owls just hoot, "Stay here for a while!"

The stars dress up, twinkling in rows,
As the night-time breeze brings comedic woes.
A hare hops along, joking with glee,
In the calm of the night, so silly and free.

Echoes of Silence Beneath the Stars

In silence echoes laughter, soft and light,
As fireflies dance, giving bugs a fright.
The moon rolls his eyes at a stars' silly trick,
While shadows sneak off, playing hide-and-seek quick.

A deer snorts a joke, while raccoons just snicker,
And the whole woods chuckle—what a quicker picker!
Under twinkling lights, the night's full of cheer,
With every soft whisper, it's clear they are near.

The Rustle of Golden Dreams

Leaves giggle as they swirl,
Cackling like a cheeky girl.
A breeze whispers, 'Look at me!'
While squirrels plot their jubilee.

In the trees, a party starts,
With branches playing funny parts.
Acorns roll, and twigs engage,
Nature's clowns set the stage.

Twilight fades, the fun won't cease,
As everyone joins in with ease.
Laughter fills the earthy floor,
Who knew dreams could be such a roar?

Golden shades glint with a glee,
While shadows play hide-and-seek, you see.
Each rustle brings a smile anew,
In this wild night, we bid adieu.

Shadows Dance on a Cool Night

Beneath the trees, shadows prance,
Like they've mastered an awkward dance.
They twirl and twist with silly glee,
Making fools of the moonlit spree.

Crickets sing a rhythm keen,
While owls show off their regal sheen.
Branches wave like hands in jest,
Nature's show is surely the best.

A raccoon steals a snack in haste,
With antics that none can outpace.
The night is full of giggly roars,
As laughter travels through open doors.

Cool winds carry whispered jokes,
As fireflies light up the folks.
A night of fun, and no regret,
With shadow guests we won't forget.

The Language of Falling Leaves

Leaves drop down with cheeky flair,
Whisper secrets in the air.
Sprinkled gold, like glitter flies,
In a play, where laughter lies.

Each leaf has tales of witty sights,
Of playful days and silly nights.
They flutter down with joyful cheers,
And tickle toes of passing peers.

The wind joins in, a jester bold,
Stirring up tales long left untold.
Rustling, chuckling, it carries forth,
A theater scene of nature's worth.

In this world, where fun never leaves,
We dance on paths made of these thieves.
With every crinkle, a joke's embraced,
As laughter in the air is traced.

Nighttime Reveries Beneath the Stars

Stars giggle in the velvet sky,
While night critters laugh and sigh.
Dreams tiptoe in with funny face,
As shadows hide in a silly race.

Crickets chatter with punchlines bold,
While fireflies twinkle like stories told.
The moon winks down with a friendly grin,
In this night's magic, we all dive in.

Each soft breeze carries a witty tune,
That dances softly under the moon.
The hour is ripe for mischief and play,
As dreams and chuckles come out to stay.

In reveries spun with laughter bright,
We find our joy in the cool night light.
Every murmur stirs a joyous spark,
In this delightful, whimsical park.

The Lure of the Twilight Thicket

In the thicket, critters dance,
Underneath the moon's fixed glance.
A raccoon slips, a squirrel trips,
While fireflies flicker in joyful quips.

Caught in laughter, they play a game,
Chasing shadows, no fear of shame.
The owl hoots as if to say,
'Oh dear friends, keep clumsiness at bay!'

The night air fills with silly sounds,
As laughter bounces off the mounds.
The fox struts with vaudeville flair,
While the mushrooms giggle—oh, the dare!

And as the sun begins to creep,
They'll finish the fun before they sleep.
So let's embrace the night so bright,
In the thicket, we feel all right!

Savoring Silence in the Whispering Woods

In the woods where whispers play,
Silence sings in a quirky way.
The owls gossip, the bees conspire,
While crickets spark their own choir.

A deer tiptoes, cautious and shy,
Stumbling onto a laughing fly.
With every buzz, a giggle stirs,
As flowers chuckle at the blurs.

Squirrels chat, their voices loud,
About acorns and chasing clouds.
And while we sit, a breeze takes flight,
It carries secrets of the night.

So pass the stories, let them flow,
In this silence, we surely glow.
Together, laughter fills the air,
In the woods, we have not a care!

Conversations in the Heart of Autumn

Amidst the leaves of orange and gold,
Stories unfold, both funny and bold.
The pumpkins sit with a smirk so wide,
As the crows caw jokes, oh, what a ride!

Chitchat flows from the chill in the air,
And rabbits hop here, unaware.
The acorns argue, who has the best hat,
While the wind just shakes its head at that!

A squirrel slips on a crispy snack,
Falling hard, oh, what a whack!
Laughter rings through the harvest cheer,
As the trees nod subtly, lending their ear.

In this season of jest and delight,
Conversations sparkle under the moonlight.
So gather 'round, let the stories unfurl,
In autumn's heart, let humor whirl!

Whispers Beneath the Canopy

Beneath the leaves where shadows drip,
Whispers float on a playful trip.
A bear sneezes, the woods erupt,
While the brook laughs and bubbles up!

The turtles share a sassy joke,
While birds sing loud, then softly croak.
Leaves chuckle as they dance and sway,
Telling tales of a sunny day.

A curious raccoon peeks from a tree,
Wondering what the fuss could be.
The owls nod, wise to the game,
Encouraging all to join the fame.

As night descends, the laughter ignites,
Under the canopy, the joy invites.
So let's whisper secrets, soft as air,
In this forest, we've nothing to spare!

Jigsaw of Stars and Leaves

In the dark, the leaves fall down,
Like puzzle pieces in a frown.
Stars giggle, twinkling bright,
As squirrels dance in the moonlight.

The trees whisper silly jokes,
While critters prance like little folks.
A raccoon puts on a silly show,
Claiming it's the best, though it's slow.

Owl wonders who's winning this game,
As fireflies flicker, but it's all the same.
They shine more brightly than the stars,
While raccoons play their air guitars.

Laughter echoes through the park,
As shadows wiggle after dark.
Nature's pranksters on a spree,
Bring giggles to the night like free.

The Golden Hour's Secret Song

As twilight paints the world in gold,
Giggling breezes, tales retold.
A chipmunk sings, oh what a voice,
He croons of nuts, he has no choice.

The sun dips low, a wobbly throne,
Birds tweet secrets, they watch alone.
A rabbit hops, quite out of tune,
While shadows dance beneath the moon.

Leaves rustle with a teasing grin,
As laughter echoes deep within.
The breeze plays notes from far-off lands,
While butterflies perform in bands.

Silly songs of the setting sun,
A chorus of laughs, oh what fun!
Under the glow, we sway and sway,
In golden hour, we laugh away.

Autumn's Gentle Humming

In the crisp air, whispers float,
Squirrels chatter, plotting notes.
A breeze hums low, oh what a sound,
As leaves pirouette, round and round.

The pumpkins chuckle, round and fat,
Telling tales of a cheeky cat.
With shadows long, they stretch and peek,
As laughter dances, loud and cheeky.

A hedgehog struts in a tiny hat,
And prancing ants debate the mat.
Fall's a stage, so full of cheer,
With costumes bright and some sincere.

Crunching leaves, a symphony plays,
Nature's jokes in funny ways.
With giggles shared on every street,
Autumn hums a song so sweet.

Ferns in a Soft Glow

Under moonlight, ferns unfold,
Whispering secrets, brave and bold.
They laugh at shadows creeping near,
In their soft glow, there's nothing to fear.

A ladybug twirls in delight,
Her polka-dot dress shining bright.
A glowworm winks, so out of place,
As crickets join the silly race.

Mossy rocks hold a giggling crew,
Hosting parties for ants anew.
With tiny cheers and tiny cakes,
They toast to all their quirky fakes.

In the glen, where dreams take flight,
Softly glowing, they share the night.
Ferns sway to their laughter's tune,
As the world dances beneath the moon.

The Lure of Dusk's Embrace

As daylight fades, the silliness grows,
In shadows where mischief quietly flows.
Bouncing squirrels with nut-shaped hats,
Dance around, ignoring the chats.

The rabbits giggle, a deer joins in,
Making up games with a cheeky grin.
Chasing fireflies, they twist and twirl,
In evening's glow, their antics unfurl.

A wise old owl hoots a witty pun,
While frogs croak jokes, just for fun.
Whispers of laughter fill the trees,
As night ticks on with a teasing breeze.

In the embrace of dusk, all seems bright,
The forest giggles, oh what a sight!
With every rustle and playful tease,
The night becomes a world of ease.

Flickers of Fireflies' Secrets

Fireflies flicker with giggles at night,
Their tiny bulbs twinkle, oh what a sight!
They whisper secrets as they zoom around,
Making sure no one hears a sound.

With a flick and a blink, they draw us near,
Telling tales of mischief without fear.
A beetle joins in, cracking a joke,
And the moths laugh till they nearly choke.

In the moonlit chaos, they swirl and swirl,
Creating a dance with a sparkly whirl.
Their glowing laughter lights up the dark,
While crickets chirp, keeping up the spark.

A luminous party, with wild delight,
Where critters gather to share the night.
As stars wink down, the fun won't cease,
In the glow of secrets, they find their peace.

Chants from the Understory

In the deep woods, a chorus starts,
Where critters gather with laughter in parts.
Raccoons wearing masks lead the tune,
While owls crack jokes beneath the moon.

A hedgehog hums with a prickly flair,
Join in the song, no need to despair!
The fungi bob along, swaying low,
Mushroom dancers, putting on a show.

They sing of acorns and sunny delight,
Of mischief brewed in the cool of night.
Each verse a classic, a tale so bright,
Laughter and tunes make everything right.

So join the throng in this leafy spree,
With every chant, there's giggles aplenty.
In the understory, the world is fun,
Where nature's party has just begun.

Echoes of Ember and Leaf

The crackling fire sends smoke signals high,
While critters roast marshmallows, oh me, oh my!
A chipmunk complains, 'I've burned my paw!'
While the wise old fox just laughs and guffaws.

Leaves snap underfoot like comedy acts,
As raccoons stage heists, planning their pacts.
With every rustle, they share a jest,
And even the skunks seem to laugh the best!

A badger joins in with a comical tale,
Of running from crows and a giant snail!
They squeal and they roll in a heap on the ground,
Making sure every funny moment is found.

In the light of embers, fun stories blend,
The forest united, with giggles to send.
Echoes of laughter, a festive leaf,
Replaying the joy, chased away the grief.

Silent Echoes of Dusk's Palette

In the twilight's embrace, we gather near,
Crayons arguing, 'Who's the best here?'
Orange claims the sky, while purple gets sassy,
Green rolls its eyes, saying, 'You're too flashy!'

A picnic of laughter spreads across the lawn,
Chips and giggles are hilariously drawn.
The fireflies dance as if in a race,
While shadows play tag, laughing in grace.

Dreaming in the Depths of Twilight

Beneath the stars, dreams take a flight,
Socks on our heads, what a silly sight!
Aliens are coming, or so we declare,
With carrots for noses, they won't seem rare!

Pillow fights swell, like cotton clouds rise,
"Is this real life?" we question with eyes.
Giggling whispers echo through the night,
As dawn hears our secrets, bursting with light!

Beneath the Boughs of Night

Under the trees, where owls hoot with glee,
A raccoon wears glasses, just look and see!
Squirrels in tuxedos, dancing away,
Debating who's fancier, a nut or a tray!

Night's canvas is painted with wacky delight,
As ladybugs gossip, taking flight.
The moon, it chuckles, glowing so bright,
"Is this a party? Oh, what a sight!"

Murmurs in the Moonlit Wilderness

The woods talk softly, in whispers and tunes,
A hedgehog sings opera, beneath silver moons.
Rabbits discuss, who can jump the highest,
While frogs croak complaints, grading the bias.

In this moonlit chaos, jokes take their turn,
As butterflies giggle, and lanterns all burn.
Each twig plays a part in night's endless jest,
With shadows as actors, it's laughter, not rest!

Celestial Breezes and Barking Moonlight

The stars are out, they wink and blink,
The moon's a dog, it loves to stink.
Breezes whisper, teasing the leaves,
As shadows dance, oh, what a tease!

The crickets croon a silly song,
While owls hoot all night long.
A squirrel prances in a hat,
He thinks he's cool – imagine that!

The fireflies flash their disco lights,
In this crazy scene, all's alright!
With laughter bubbling in the air,
The midnight fun spreads everywhere.

And as we twirl beneath the sky,
I trip and fall, you laugh and cry.
In moonlit games, our joy ignites,
A symphony of silly delights.

Ephemeral Shadows of Twilight

The twilight casts a playful shade,
Where shadows leap, no plans are laid.
A cat wears glasses, thinks it's wise,
While owls take notes, with watchful eyes.

They debate if stars are made of cheese,
And how to tickle gentle breeze.
The moon's a comedian, cracking jokes,
As fireflies buzz, the night's own folks.

A raccoon juggles shiny spoons,
The laughs echo beneath the moon.
Whispers of silliness fill the glade,
In twilight's glow, our worries fade.

The shadows hold a secret cheer,
With giggles shared, there's naught to fear.
Together we caper, twirl, and sway,
In this ephemeral nighttime play.

The Secret Garden's Evening Play

In the secret garden, mischief brews,
With flowers that dance in silly shoes.
They giggle softly, sharing their tease,
While frogs wear crowns beneath the trees.

A gnome cracks jokes that no one gets,
Heroic squirrels in fuzzy vests.
The moon chuckles, sipping sweet tea,
As petals flutter, oh, so carefree!

Bunnies bounce in a hopscotch game,
They gently giggle, calling your name.
The night is ripe with giddy delight,
In this playful patch, everything's bright.

So come along, let laughter soar,
In this garden's heart, there's fun galore.
With secrets spun and joy in sway,
Join the whimsical evening play.

Amber Glows and Twilight Blues

Amber glow drapes the world in cheer,
As twilight giggles, coming near.
The sun's yawning, with sleepy eyes,
Saying goodbye to all the skies.

Bats perform their aerial dance,
While raccoons stare with a sideways glance.
A moose on skates glides by with flair,
Causing a ruckus in the air!

The fireflies play tag in loops,
While owls drop in, like curious troops.
The night fills with contagious grins,
As laughter melts away our sins.

In amber hues, our spirits rise,
Under a canvas of twilight skies.
With jests and jabs, the world feels new,
In this quirky night, just me and you.

The Soft Serenade of Fallen Foliage

Leaves whisper tales of playful dreams,
They tumble down in silly streams.
Squirrels giggle in the twirling gusts,
While acorns plot their tiny rusts.

Crickets make jokes with chirps so bright,
Underneath the starlit night.
A raccoon prances with a cheeky grin,
As shadows dance and softly spin.

The breeze becomes a jester's song,
Where every twig can do no wrong.
Fallen foliage sways with glee,
In this forest jubilee.

So come and join this leafy choir,
With laughter that will never tire.
In rustling leaves, joy comes alive,
As nature's humor starts to thrive.

Shadows Dancing on the Forest Floor

Underneath the moon's round face,
Shadows boogie with graceful pace.
Branches wiggle in the night,
While owls hoot in pure delight.

Beneath the stars, a laughter gale,
Every critter tells a tale.
Bunnies hop and stomp in time,
With a rhythm that feels sublime.

The rustling rusts bring giggles near,
As night critters shift and leer.
A hedgehog slips, does a funny roll,
In this wild and whimsical stroll.

Join the dance of shadows bold,
In every creak, a secret told.
The forest floor, a stage of cheer,
Where laughter blooms, year after year.

Nighttime Chronicles of the Rustling Trees

The trees hold secrets, giggles and sighs,
A raucous party beneath the skies.
Branches rustle, sharing their jokes,
While fireflies wink like playful folks.

The owls share wisdom, but with a twist,
A joke about squirrels that can't be missed.
Leaves shiver and shake with delight,
In the comedic dance of the night.

Foxes chuckle, tails held high,
As moonbeams wink from way up high.
Every crunch underfoot makes them laugh,
In this nocturnal, joyful path.

So listen close to the night's own grin,
Where every rustle invites you in.
The trees are alive with tales so funny,
As the nighttime wraps us in its honey.

Lullabies Hushed by the Moonlight

Once upon a time in a cozy nook,
The critters gathered, each with a book.
With whispers soft as a feather's kiss,
They'd share their tales, all filled with bliss.

A snail creeps up, slow and steady,
With a silly story, always ready.
The raccoon adds a twist with flair,
As laughter fills the chilled night air.

The shadows weave a tapestry grand,
Where gaily chuckling creatures stand.
Each lullaby kissed by playful glee,
In moonlight's glow, they sing so free.

So nestle in and close your eyes tight,
Dream of giggles dancing in the night.
In this realm of humor, sleep draws near,
With lullabies only creatures hear.

Moonlit Leaves in Conversation

Under the moon's watchful gaze,
Leaves chatter softly, in playful ways.
They gossip of squirrels, in cheeky delight,
While shadows dance, in the cool night light.

A branch whines about losing a twig,
That landed on the back of a dancing pig.
"Did you hear?" whispers one to another,
"They're stealing our beauty, the shimmery brother!"

The stars giggle at leafy tales spun,
As crickets hold court, the night's jester fun.
Each rustle a pun, each flicker a jest,
In this woodland theater, they're surely the best.

So join in the chatter, if you pass by,
Where leaves wear their humor like stars in the sky.
Together they weave a tapestry bright,
Of laughter and giggles beneath the moonlight.

Secrets Sway in the Silent Breeze

In the hush of the night, secrets float light,
The breeze lies in wait, holding laughter tight.
It whispers of acorns with dreams that they found,
And the tales of the critters that dance on the ground.

A raccoon with a hat, quite quirky and round,
Claims to visit the moon, where lost socks abound.
The branches shake lightly, as if sharing a joke,
While shadows behind them play peek-a-boak.

"Did you see the owl?" a leaf flutters bold,
"He forgot where he perched, poor old bird turned cold!"
With chuckles that sparkle like dew on the grass,
They bond in the night, as their worries the pass.

In this giggly realm, with stories galore,
The secrets they keep, make them want to explore.
So listen and laugh, in the stillness so deep,
For the night holds its humor, in whispers they keep.

Echoes of Autumn's Embrace

In amber glow, autumn plays tricks,
As leaves fall like laughter, a quirky mix.
They tumble and twirl, with no care for the ground,
While acorns say, "Hey, we're best all around!"

A ghost of a tree, blending in the fun,
Swings his branches like arms, a dance just begun.
The wind gets confused, tickles bark with a tease,
"Hold your bark tight, or you'll blow with the breeze!"

The pumpkins all chuckle, with faces painted bright,
"Mistake me for candy? Oh, what a delight!"
While shadows join in, with a waltz on the ground,
Creating a riddle of joy all around.

So gather your laughter, as leaves sing their tune,
For autumn is here, under the watchful moon.
Echoes of joy, in this playful embrace,
Remind us that nature holds magic in space.

Nocturnal Serenade of the Woods

Underneath the stars, a frog hits a note,
While fireflies join, in a glowing little boat.
"Ribbit your way to fame!" they cheer and they croon,
As owls hoot the rhythm, of a funky cartoon.

A trio of raccoons with hats made of leaves,
Breakdance on the turf, while the moon quietly grieves.
The trees sway in time, as if on a spree,
"Watch the moves, my friends, come dance along with me!"

Jays tease the night with sweet chirps and pranks,
Leave the other critters in a fit of their ranks.
"Who's got the beat?" a badger yells out,
But the night keeps on dancing, giggles abound.

So let's join the song, as the woods come alive,
With laughter and joy, as the critters all thrive.
In this nocturnal caper, where fun takes its flight,
We find merriment hidden, in the heart of the night.

The Language of the Forest's Heart

The trees whisper secrets, oh so bright,
Chirping squirrels giggle with delight.
Leaves play hide and seek in the breeze,
While owls hoot riddles among the trees.

Mushrooms wear hats, looking quite spry,
As fireflies dance in the darkening sky.
Rabbits crack jokes with their twitching tails,
And crickets tell stories that never fail.

The moon joins in with a chuckling glow,
As shadows perform in their twilight show.
Running through moments, the laughter ensues,
Nature's odd humor, it always bemuse.

In the forest's heart where the wild things play,
Every leaf has a quip, in its own funny way.
So listen closely, keep your ears near,
For each rustle and giggle is what you will hear.

Tumbling Thoughts of an Autumn Night

As autumn winds swirl and twist around,
Thoughts leap like children, making a sound.
Ghostly pumpkins who chuckle and grin,
Invite all the creatures for a whimsical spin.

The moon is a jester, draped in a gown,
While starlit squirrels hold a nutty showdown.
Leaves tumble down with a comical flair,
Each one a performer, floating through air.

A raccoon with mischief in his bright eyes,
Dances with shadows, stealing the prize.
Cotton candy clouds drift in playful pairs,
Tickling the night with whimsical flares.

So if you wander, look closely and see,
The giggling rustles of nighttime glee.
From whispers of trees to the moon up so high,
Every moment is laughter beneath the sky.

The Timelessness of Twinkling Leaves

In the crisp air, leaves start their hum,
Tickling the branches, oh what fun!
Bouncing in circles, they twirl with grace,
In a wacky waltz, they find their place.

A breeze tells jokes, tickling the ground,
While pine needles giggle, making a sound.
Fluttering down, the leaves take their flight,
Dressed in colors, they shine in the night.

Squirrels with acorns hold a grand show,
Puppets of nature, stealing the glow.
Pattering paws chase whispers around,
In the timeless dance, joy can be found.

So gather your smiles, come join in the spree,
For the forest's a stage, just wait and see.
In this playful world where all things believe,
Laughter's the language, taught by the leaves.

www.ingramcontent.com/pod-product-compliance
Lightning Source LLC
Chambersburg PA
CBHW071828160426
43209CB00003B/242